The Story of
CORNWALL

S. Daniell

Tor Mark Press • Redruth

Engine house at Trewavas Head, west of Porthleven

Second edition published 1989 by Tor Mark Press,
United Downs Industrial Estate, St Day, Redruth, Cornwall TR16 5HY

This reprint 1998

ISBN 0-85025-309-8

Acknowledgements
The publishers are grateful to the following for their kind permission to reproduce illustrations:
Cornwall Local Studies Library, Redruth, pages 22 and 24; Men-an-Tol Studio page 12; Royal Institution of Cornwall pages 1, 28, 31, 33, 35, 36, 37 and 39; Paul White pages 2, 5, 6, 14, 17 and 19. The cover illustration is by Roger Lavis. The publishers are also grateful to Roger Penhallurick for his assistance with the picture research.

Printed in Great Britain by Burstwick Print & Publicity Services, Hull

1

The Stone and Bronze Ages

The first inhabitants of Cornwall were hunters and food gatherers who lived, along with such creatures as mammoths and sabre-toothed tigers, on the southern margins of the ice-sheets which covered much of Europe during the great Ice Age. In Britain the ice reached as far south as the Thames and the Severn, so that the south-west peninsula for half a million years resembled the lands in which the Eskimo lives today; stony, barren and bitterly cold. These Old Stone Age or Paleolithic men, tall, rugged and with massive jaws and brows, have left few traces of their way of life. This is mainly because they had no control over their environment and neither ploughed the land, herded animals nor made permanent dwellings. Nevertheless, it has long been known that a number inhabited Kent's Cavern near Torquay about 14,000 years ago, towards the end of the Ice Age, and several ancient hearths with burnt bones of about the same period have been discovered at Praa Sands, near Marazion. Crude tools, made by chipping and flaking pieces of flint taken from the beaches, have been found at Godrevy near Hayle. These are of a later date by several thousands of years, their owners living at a time when the ice sheets were finally melting and withdrawing towards the North Pole.

The increasing warmth of climate which brought this about also caused the gradual spread of forests, firstly pine, birch and willow, then oak, except on the higher land, where in Cornwall the extensive peat bogs of the moors began to form. Old Stone Age man, who was a hunter and had ranged widely over the open ground south of the ice in Europe, gradually gave way to Mesolithic man. In Cornwall, these people lived in small groups chiefly around the coast and were probably less nomadic. It is likely that they existed by fishing, by collecting shellfish, nuts and berries or by snaring small animals and birds, all within a restricted locality. Still no attempt was made to till the soil or herd animals for the sake of convenience. Neither, so far as is known, were any permanent dwellings made or the crafts of pottery making or weaving practised. These Mesolithic peoples inhabited Cornwall from about 5000 to 2000 B.C., a few eking out their existence on the open moors, as around Dozmary Pool on Bodmin Moor, but most of them were concentrated on the north coast. It is known, for instance, that some lived along the Land's End cliffs, on the Camel estuary and at Gwithian, near Hayle. Traces of their cooking hearths have been found as well as many of the tiny flint blades which they fashioned and the chipping floors where this work was done. These blades, each about half an inch long, were mounted along a grooved wooden shaft to give a saw-toothed edge.

The melting of the ice sheets caused a gradual rise in sea-level, cutting Britain off from Europe about 6500 B.C. Thus it was that when New Stone Age or Neolithic people arrived in this country they came by sea from the Continent, reaching these shores about 3000 B.C. – a time when the rich and complex civilisation of ancient Egypt was at its height. These people, small and agile, were infinitely superior culturally to the Mesolithic food gatherers and hunters already in occupation, for they were not only growers of grain and herders of animals but also made cloth and pottery. They also, of course, had boats capable of carrying them and their farm stock and seed corn across the Channel. They also produced very fine polished tools, including axes of flint or, in Cornwall, of greenstone, a rock similar to granite and common in the county.

In order to farm they made forest clearings with these axes, at the same time establishing an important coastal and overland trade with other parts of Britain. Their axes were manufactured at various places in Cornwall, including sites near Camborne, Cape Cornwall, St. Ives, Marazion and Mousehole. Only one New Stone Age settlement site has so far been discovered, on the south-east side of Carn Brea, near Camborne, with another probable dwelling site at Gwithian. Flint axes, leaf-shaped arrowheads and pottery have been found at each, while Gwithian also revealed Mesolithic tools which had been re-worked, using the improved New Stone Age techniques.

More fascinating perhaps than these traces of activity and occupation are the henge monuments of Cornwall which were

Dozmary Pool, near Jamaica Inn, was a Mesolithic site; it is also claimed in legend as the place where Sir Bedivere threw away King Arthur's sword

constructed during the period when the Stone Age was merging into the Bronze Age, about 1800 B.C. These great oval or circular earthworks, comprising a ditch within a bank, were used for purposes unknown today, although it is perhaps not unreasonable to imagine a religious ceremony taking place there, with spectators seated on the surrounding bank; the best known of the Cornish henges is at Castilly, near Lanivet. Some henges outside Cornwall contain stone circles or settings, Stonehenge for instance: one example, the Stripple Stones, occurs on Bodmin Moor. The building of Cornwall's many other stone circles commenced some time during the same period and continued until about 900 B.C. Usually with about twenty or so granite stones set upright, they are found chiefly on Bodmin Moor, for example the Hurlers: or Land's End region, the well-known Merry Maidens near Lamorna. Again, their purpose can only be surmised. Their erection commenced about the same time as those other interesting Bronze Age monuments, the solitary granite pillars called menhirs (Cornish, *men*-stone; *hyr*-long) of which there are many in the county. Two massive examples occur together near the Merry Maidens and are known as the Pipers; more recent folk-lore claims that the girls and their musicians were petrified for dancing on the Sabbath. In fact, it is likely that

Trethevy Quoit on the southern edge of Bodmin Moor.

menhirs were memorials or even gravestones; several set up in the late Bronze Age are known to be associated with burial.

The beginnings of the Bronze Age in Cornwall, as elsewhere in England, were remarkable for the arrival from the Continent of small groups of Beaker people, so called because of their sophisticated pottery beakers. They mainly used stone tools and weapons but knew how to make others of copper or bronze and in that respect differed from the earlier inhabitants. They also differed from them in their practice of individual burial under small round barrows, usually little over two feet high. This type of single grave was to become typical of Bronze Age peoples, although at a later date cremation became more usual than inhumation. These round Bronze Age barrows are extremely numerous in Cornwall – almost 900 are known – and show considerable variety in design and burial practice. Sometimes, for instance, the cremated bones or ashes were placed in a large urn, sometimes in a cist; and occasionally the large barrows are grouped together in a cemetery, like the ten found at Pelynt, near Looe, which date from about 1500 B.C.

The Beaker people were a mobile warrior-hunter people, enterprising and resourceful, quite different from the settled New Stone Age farmers they came amongst. In particular they initiated and encouraged trade, which brought about the spread of metallurgy and the beginning of the Bronze Age in England. Commerce between Ireland, where there was gold and copper, and the Continent crossed the Cornish peninsula itself. Gold ingots, jewellery and crescent necklaces from Ireland have been found in Cornwall as a result of these contacts, as well as beads from the eastern Mediterranean.

The prosperity resulting from the early Bronze Age trade is reflected in the fine bronze daggers and the unique gold cup of Aegean design found in Cornish graves of the period.

Bronze Age settlements must have been widespread in Cornwall but now naturally little remains of them except in remote areas. On Bodmin Moor are many dwellings, remains of pastoral communities who lived in groups of round, stone-walled huts, with roofs probably raftered and thatched. The houses were either linked by a series of protective walls or totally enclosed within a pound. On the lower ground it is likely that more arable farming was practised and at Gwithian marks of ploughing have been found, the earliest known in Britain.

Set up by an entirely different people arriving by sea during the late Stone/early Bronze Age are the great stone tombs of the far west of Cornwall. Some of these comprise a massive granite capstone set across several vertical slabs, like a giant table. Originally they contained communal inhumations in the Stone Age tradition and were covered by large barrows or cairns of earth and stone; Lanyon Quoit and Chun Quoit in the Land's End are good examples. There is also another type formed like a dead-end tunnel roofed and walled with stone, and again originally covered with a mound. There are over forty of these in Scilly and about a third of this number in the Land's End, the most remarkable being Ballowal Carn near Cape Cornwall.

2

The Iron Age and the Romans

The Iron age came to Britain with the first of several waves of immigrant peoples from the Continent, reaching Cornwall about 500 B.C. Here they settled on all but the highest moorlands, where the Bronze Age peoples to some extent still remained but where life was becoming less and less attractive due to a gradual deterioration in climate. Increasing cold and damp made living conditions on an area like Bodmin Moor most unpleasant, and caused further expansion of the large peat bogs.

These newcomers to Britain, tall, strong and clannish by nature, were Celtic speaking, unlike their Stone and Bronze Age predecessors. They were, moreover, expert warriors, familiar with the working of iron, equipped with iron swords and other weapons as well as iron tools. All of these were far more effective than any made of bronze and moreover were made more easily and cheaply. To those already settled in the peninsula of Cornwall, the Celts must have appeared an aggressive people, for they were organised into tribes under warrior chiefs and spent a considerable amount of time in a struggle to acquire territory one from the other, as well as in the building of numerous fortifications.

One of the earliest of these forts, which was built by the first wave of Celts who settled on the north coast, is Maen Castle above Sennen Cove. Here a dry-stone wall was constructed across the neck of a promontory and behind this it was possible to retreat in times of danger. When successive waves of Celtic immigrants arrived, especially in the 3rd and 2nd centuries B.C., the number and variety of fortifications rapidly increased, and traces of these are to be found throughout the county. The types range from a single bank and ditch surrounding a small farmstead or hamlet, covering perhaps two acres, to great tribal hill top forts up to six or seven times this in area and protected by one or more closely spaced ramparts of earth of stone. Castle-an-Dinas overlooking Goss Moor, Carn Brea above Redruth and Trencrom near St. Ives are of this type and occupy strategic positions. Dozens of fine promontory forts were also constructed, each commanding wide stretches of coastline and generally built on a grander scale than the earlier Maen Castle; outstanding examples are the quadruple-ramparted fort on Trevelgue Head, near Newquay, those with three ramparts on Gurnard's Head west of St. Ives, and The Rumps, north of the Camel estuary. There are also numbers of so-called forts built in less strategic positions on the slopes of hills; their widely spaced protective banks seem to be more for enclosure and shelter of beasts than for defensive purposes; earthworks of this kind occur close together at Gear and Caervallack on the Helford River. In a few of these numerous and varied 'forts', signs of permanent habitation have been found, and it is probable that the major ones, either on the hills or the coastal headlands, were the dwellings and headquarters of tribal chieftains; the famous site of Castle Dore, near Fowey, although not very large, was certainly so occupied by a community, perhaps with its tribal leader.

A great deal has been learned about the Iron Age inhabitants of Cornwall from excavations of several of the 'forts', as well as other places. Moreover, two Iron Age cemeteries have been discovered, one made by the early Celtic invaders who had a settlement beside their burial ground at Harlyn Bay near Padstow and another of later date at Trelan Bahow near St. Keverne in the Lizard. In the former, well over a hundred graves were opened, revealing skeletons in coffins made of slate slabs, several of which can still be inspected in the grounds of a museum on the site. The bodies, wearing personal ornaments, were interred with knees drawn up to the chin and skull fractured – the latter perhaps to allow the escape of their spirits. None had been cremated and no grave was marked by either cairn or mound – altogether a totally different burial practice from that of the Bronze Age peoples. At Trelan Bahow, the grave goods were more elaborate and showed that the women of the tribe had a greater social standing than was the case in more primitive communities; as well as jewellery, one possessed an elegant bronze mirror with a beautifully engraved back. Other grave goods, as well as many finds within the different types of forts, show these Iron Age people to have been dwellers in stone-walled or timber huts, to have reared sheep and cattle, grown corn in small fields, to have been familiar with the working of leather, as well as the spinning, weaving and possibly dyeing of cloth. The making of pottery was also known, not only by hand but also upon a wheel, and pots were sometimes decorated elaborately with incised scrolls, with cordons, or even stamped with patterns of ducks. Other finds on occupation sites include metallic ores of tin, copper and iron – none of which were mined, of course, but obtained from surface deposits – and indications of the smelting and working of these metals including crucibles, moulds and ingots as well as intricately worked articles in bronze, sometimes set with enamel and glass, and tools and weapons of iron. In fact these Celts were already engaged in the trading of tin from Cornwall across France to the Mediterranean before they came to the county, a trade which flourished from about the fifth century until the conquest of Gaul (France) by Julius Caesar about 60 B.C. There is still in existence an H-shaped ingot of tin weighing 158 pounds of the type made by these people. It was dredged up in Falmouth harbour and was no doubt intended for the Mediterranean market at this time, although St. Michael's Mount appears to have been the principal point of shipment.

The invasion of Gaul by Caesar's armies drove the last wave of Celts across Britain as far as Cornwall as refugees, and it was possibly the knowledge that Roman armies had crossed the Channel about 100 years later, after Gaul was finally conquered, that caused at least one Celtic fort in the county to be further strengthened about this time. But in fact the Romans were to have relatively little effect upon the extreme south-west, just as they made little or no impression on those other remote and more mountainous parts of these islands, namely Scotland, Wales and Ireland. Wales and Scotland became military zones, the frontiers of which were guarded by Roman legions whose task it was to contain those tribes – savage no doubt in Roman eyes – which had taken refuge there. South-eastern England, in all respects more attractive to the Romans, became a civil zone of administration while Cornwall, neither so inhospitable nor so rebellious as Wales and the wilds of Scotland, played what might be regarded as a more intermediary role. The Romans must have been interested in both her alluvial tin and her deposits of iron ore.

The inhabitants of the county, Celts and pre-Celts, now known as the Dumnonii, were allowed a large measure of self government, in common with much of the rest of the Roman province of Britain. Governed from the newly founded Roman town of Exeter, where Celtic tribal chieftains of the Roman canton of the south-west met and conferred, they enjoyed some of the benefits of Roman rule, although of course not without taxation as a result. It is probable, for instance, that three roads were built in the county, perhaps on account of the trade in tin, for Roman milestones have been found at Boscastle and Tintagel; St. Hilary and Breage; and near Redruth. One Roman villa has been discovered at Magor, near Camborne which, although not of a very high standard compared to the many fine villas of south-east England, has a mosaic floor, tiled roof and painted, plastered walls. A two-acre Roman fort has also been excavated, guarding a crossing of the Camel at Nanstallon, near Bodmin. It was rectangular in plan, unlike those of earlier peoples, and was equipped with workshops, barracks and good roads within the defences. Two other Roman forts are known to exist in Cornwall and it is probable that there are yet more.

Because the Celtic population of Cornwall was mainly left to its own devices, the more primitive mode of life of these peoples largely continued under Roman rule. A small settlement at Gwithian, for instance, continued undisturbed in its use largely of weapons and tools of stone. The great Iron Age camp on Carn Brea, looking out towards the north cliffs over the Roman villa at Magor was also in occupation, as was the large cliff castle of Trevelgue. So too was the fort of Carloggas near Newquay and the better known Castle Dore north of Fowey, together with several smaller sites. Most interesting among these are the courtyard-house villages of the Land's End peninsula. These clustered settlements, of which about forty have been located, came into being about 25 A.D. and some were occupied until the fifth century. Each comprises a number of oval, stone-walled houses in which the rooms open out on to a central courtyard. A fine example is found at Porthmeor, while at Chysauster, the best known of these villages, eight houses lies on either side of a street with their backs turned against the south-west wind. In each dwelling there is a workshop, a living room and a stable, while

An Iron Age hut, which would have been roofed with branches and turf or thatch

outside there is a small garden plot. There are also terraced fields, and conduits bringing water into the settlement. Another interesting feature of these villages, as well as of certain Iron Age forts, is the fogou, a long underground passage lined with granite. This was used, it is believed, for the cold storage of food, but some may have served the purpose of a refuge or even have had religious significance.

3

The Dark Ages and the Cornish Saints

In 410 A.D., with unruly tribes encroaching on the boundaries of the Empire, the power of Rome was in decline to such an extent that her legions were withdrawn from Britain, leaving the country to organise its own defences against possible invaders. Forty years later, heathen Anglo-Saxons – basically the English people – migrated to eastern England from the Continent, a tall, fair warrior people intent on destroying all traces of civilisation as they progressed, as well as the Christian faith which the Romans had introduced into Britain in the fourth century. These troubled centuries, of which few records exist, are known as the Dark Ages.

Before the advancing Anglo-Saxons, many Romano-British people fled into Wales or the south-west peninsula and by the beginning of the sixth century the Celts of both areas were cut off even from each other. Thereafter the Celtic languages of these two regions gradually evolved along different lines, while in eastern England Anglo-Saxon became the customary tongue. In the remote west, too, Christianity survived among these peoples determined not to be conquered by the heathen English and who succeeded in remaining so until the ninth century. By this date, however, the English themselves had been converted to Christianity – after the landing of St. Augustine in Kent in 597 – but during the intervening centuries the Celtic form of the faith had survived only in the far west of Britain, including Cornwall.

In this period during which Cornwall resisted the Anglo-Saxons, and indeed in the period after the submission of the county, life must have continued much as it had been under the Romans. Not a great deal is known about the way in which the people lived at this time, although a number of Iron Age sites show signs of continued occupation, such as Chun Castle, the hill fort near Morvah, and Castle Dore near Fowey, as well as a new settlement of round, turf-walled huts at Gwithian.

Some of the most interesting archaeological remains belonging to this period in Cornish history are the various

This memorial stone, north of Liskeard, is elaborately inscribed for the soul of ninth century King Doniert

inscribed memorial stones scattered throughout the county. These monuments are almost certainly a continuation of the Bronze Age menhir tradition, although the latter are, of course, much larger and in no way inscribed. Characteristically these memorial stones of early Christian Cornwall occur not in groups or cemeteries but singly throughout the countryside, and they are of two types. Firstly there are those probably erected by Irish immigrants to Cornwall from Wales during the fifth century, after the withdrawl of the Romans; they may be distinguished by inscriptions in the Ogham alphabet – incised lines along the edges of the stones – which originated in Ireland some two centuries before. These stones occur mostly in the Tintagel area. More common, however, are memorial stones inscribed in Latin – often faulty Latin – and erected during the sixth and seventh centuries presumably to Celtic tribal chieftains in Cornwall. The use of this official language of the Christian church, as well as the occasional incision of the Chi-Rho monogram (formed of the letters XP, meaning Christ), indicates that these chiefs were Christians. The best known of these stones is the Men Scryfa (Stone of Writing) on the Land's End moors. This is inscribed to 'Rialobranus, son of Cunovalus', the former name meaning 'Royal Raven',the latter possibly 'Famous Prince'. A few of these Latin inscriptions are to Irish men, while at Lewannick are two stones bearing both Latin and Ogham lettering.

Undoubtedly the most romantic of these memorials lies near Castle Dore. This sixth century stone commemorates 'Drustans, son of Cunomorus', who have been identified as Tristan and King Mark of the Tristan and Iseult legend. Castle Dore, originally an Iron Age fort, it is now believed was Mark's fortress, he being one of the Cornish tribal chieftains and probably an enemy of the Irish settlers in the north. It was perhaps against their advance that the famous 'Giant's Hedge' earthwork from Lerryn to Looe was built. Even more interesting than the Tristan stone would be the discovery of one erected to King Arthur, that half legendary hero whom the Cornish have always believed led their resistance to the Anglo-Saxons during the Dark Ages. Other Celtic countries lay claim to him, but Cornwall is full of references to Arthur and his exploits, both in place-names and story, especially Tintagel Castle. In fact this was not built until the twelfth century, some six hundred years after his death, but a monastery existed there during the Dark Ages and this he may well have known.

The Tintagel Monastery, erected in the sixth century probably by Irish missionaries from Wales, was one of almost a hundred such early religious settlements in Cornwall associated with the Celtic church. Others of importance were those founded at St. Kew, Padstow, Bodmin and St. Germans, and doubtless these monasteries like that at Tintagel were very simple settlements where the monks lived in crudely built and thatched huts or 'cells' around their oratory or chapel. From such centres the missionary monks went out among a population still largely pagan on their task of conversion.

During the Dark Ages hundreds of such missionaries came to Cornwall from Ireland, Brittany and Wales, anxious to strengthen the Church in Cornwall against the incursions of heathen English. 'The Lives of the Saints', copies of which were preserved in the monasteries until the Reformation, contained much about these people, men and women, who came to Cornwall from the sixth to the ninth centuries and founded most of her churches. Today each one of these still bears the name of its founder and in this respect the churches of Cornwall are quite different from those elsewhere in England which are usually dedicated to one of the apostles. Generally speaking the Breton saints appear to have landed and settled along the southern coast of the county, the Welsh or Irish-Welsh along the north and the Irish chiefly in the extreme south-west. The saints Breaca, Ia, Germochus, Gwithianus and Wynnerus for instance, are commemorated in the parishes of Breage, St. Ives, Germoe, Gwithian and Gwinear. On the north coast near Padstow, St. Sampson is said to have landed from Wales; there is in existence an account of his missionary journey inland and his conversions of pagans whom he found worshipping a stone idol. Also landing in the same locality was St. Petroc, who founded the monasteries at Padstow and Bodmin. The best known of all the Irish Saints, however, is St. Piran who arrived near Perranporth from across the sea, floating on a millstone according to legend. Near the shore, St. Piran set up an oratory. These buildings were often erected near a spring already worshipped by the pagans and there the saint would teach and pray before those who would listen to him, converting all he could and baptising them in the water of the adjacent spring. These early chapels were usually of timber and have not survived the passage of time, although the tiny stone oratory of St. Piran at Perranporth must be very ancient. Now alas it has been reburied to protect it from vandalism. Another oratory of similar date exists at Gwithian, both having been preserved for long centuries by burial beneath blown sand. There are also to be found in Cornwall about a hundred holy wells or baptisteries, each dedicated to one of these early saints; many were regarded until quite recently as possessing special healing or prophetic powers.

Another feature of the Dark Ages in Cornwall which has come down to us is the Cornish cross, of which about 400 still exist. Most of these are of the wheel or round-headed design. The first of these Christian monuments were set up by the

Celtic cross in the churchyard of St Dennis, north of St Austell. Curiously there was no such saint: dinas *is the Cornish work for a hill-fort, and the shape of the fort is still visible*

Celtic missionaries near their chapels, like that of St. Piran, while others later were erected along paths leading to churches, at crossroads and along parish boundaries. It is quite likely that of the many known today some started off their lives as menhirs; certainly that in St. Clement's churchyard, near Truro, was originally an inscribed memorial stone of an earlier period.

4

The Middle Ages

William, Duke of Normandy, defeated King Harold and the English at the Battle of Hastings in 1066 and two years later advanced on the city of Exeter, which he captured. Thereafter Cornwall capitulated and by 1072 the whole of England had submitted to the Normans. Throughout the land large estates were granted by the Conqueror to his favourite nobles in return for military services and in the case of Cornwall over two thirds of the county fell into the hands of his half-brother Robert, Count of Mortain. Robert, together with his various sub-tenants, set about building a number of impressive castles; at Launceston, which he chose as his administrative centre, he erected the massive stronghold which came to be known as 'Castle Terrible', while amongst his other forts was that at Trematon near St. Germans, commanding the Tamar estuary. There was also the magnificent castle of Restormel, near which Lostwithiel grew up. All three were circular in plan. At a later date, the fourth of Cornwall's great castles, Tintagel, was built close to the Celtic monastery. Neither Robert nor his son William cared much for Cornwall or their castles, however, being absentee landlords who impoverished their estates. Yet worse days were to follow during the civil wars in the reign of Stephen, last of the Norman kings; then a number of smaller castles were built by the peasantry for rebel barons, under threat of extortion and torture. Among them were those at Truro and Kilkhampton, but once law and order returned to the country almost all were destroyed by command of the king.

When the Normans came to Cornwall, there were no real towns in the county at all, unless one counts the settlement around Bodmin priory, for the Celts were not by nature even villagers, let alone town dwellers. But during the years that followed a number of towns were founded by landowners who hoped to benefit from the trade, markets, fairs and the like which would follow; these towns were chiefly populated by foreigners in their early years, particularly those near the coast, like Penryn. Penryn, Helston, Lostwithiel, Launceston,

Bodmin and Liskeard became charter towns in the thirteenth century, Truro having received its charter as early as 1132. These ancient settlements still all survive as urban centres, although in most cases their *raisons d'être* – the castle, the priory, the tidal waters deep enough for ships of the day – are now a part of the past. On the other hand, many early mediaeval towns, such as Grampound, Tregoney and Mitchell, have become little more than rural backwaters.

In addition to the introduction of castles and towns into Cornwall, the Normans were great church builders. William himself was deeply religious and determined to reform the English church. Usually the earlier chapels of the saints were dispensed with and building began afresh on the same site, regardless of the fact that this was often in a remote spot beside a holy well. The types of church erected varied in both style and size. There was, for instance, the splendid building at St. Germans, where formerly had been the Anglo-Saxon cathedral of Cornwall and before that a Celtic monastery; at the other

Holy well at St Cleer

end of the scale were such diminutive churches as those of St. Enedoc near Rock, and Tintagel. Little now remains of Norman ecclesiastical architecture in the county, although something like three quarters of her churches contain traces of it – perhaps a thick wall, a slit of a window, massive rounded arch, drum-like pillar or, more commonly, an ancient font.

In Domesday Book, drawn up in 1086 as an aid to the taxation of estates under the Normans, no reference is made to Cornish tin, probably because it was regarded as royal property. Yet no doubt alluvial tin was still being worked, as it had been without a break since the Bronze Age. From 1198 the stream works were supervised by a warden appointed by the king, and in 1201 the first royal charter was granted to the tinworks or Stannaries. This allowed the tinners many privileges, including the ancient right of bounding, or searching for tin, on any land without intervention by the landlord. By the early fourteenth century they were also exempted from ordinary taxation and had their own Stannary courts and laws. During these years tin was obtained not from lodes but from alluvial gravels, using simple equipment such as picks, shovels and wooden bowls for bailing. In the twelfth century production was chiefly in eastern Cornwall but gradually spread westwards, mainly onto the granite uplands and in the area behind St. Austell Bay. This tin was superior in quality to the later lode tin and under the Normans was twice smelted, once in crude fashion by the tin-streamers, then again in certain towns selected by the warden. By the mid-fourteenth century, with improved techniques one smelting sufficed: It was carried out in crudely built, thatched structures called blowing-houses, of which there were scores up and down the county. The tin was then taken to be assayed and taxed at the appointed coinage towns – originally Lostwithiel, Liskeard, Bodmin, Truro and Helston – before finally being exported.

Most of the tin produced during the early Middle Ages was destined for the London pewterers or for the Continent. It was carried up-Channel in small sailing ships in the face of many dangers. Not only was there fear of shipwreck along the treacherous Cornish coast but also the chance of falling into the hands of pirate ships from the Cinque Ports of south-eastern England – ships which these ports were required to furnish to supplement the King's navy, but which they used also for more nefarious and more profitable business. During the early thirteenth century, the men of Fowey, themselves notorious for their fearlessness and daring at sea, were waging what was virtually a private war with the Cinque Ports. It was this kind of activity, together with the Cornishman's close acquaintance with the sea, which made him a particularly seasoned fighter and sailor. Moreover before mid-century, the Hundred Years War with France had begun and there was also trouble with Scotland, so that the seamen and ships of Cornish ports such as Fowey and Looe found themselves impressed into the King's service and taking part in great sea battles, while other Cornishmen fought at Crecy and Agincourt. For over a century this futile and costly series of wars continued, England repeatedly gaining and losing territory across the Channel. Cornwall, like the rest of the country, was impoverished by the great expense of maintaining the king's ships and fighting men. But for Cornwall at least there were compensations, as her more southerly ports thrived on the transport of supplies and troops across the Channel. Her seamen also undoubtedly enjoyed the prolonged years of lawlessness during which they raided cross-Channel ports, intercepted enemy shipping and brought it into harbour to plunder. Even after France and England were at peace, seamen from each country continued to plunder and fight at sea with the result that for many years retaliatory raids along the coast of Cornwall were common, as well as attacks by pirates from more distant Barbary. Cornish coastal towns were familiar with pillage and burning at the hands of the French as well as the Spanish; Fowey for instance was burned in 1378, Looe in 1405 and in 1457 Fowey again, this time by a Breton fleet. It was as a result of this raid that the town erected two blockhouses at the harbour entrance and between them slung a mighty chain.

During these exciting years the Black Prince, made first Duke of Cornwall by his father Edward III – who had started the wars by laying claim to the French throne – held magnificent court in Bordeaux and on two occasions came down to his castle at Restormel, accompanied by the knights who had fought alongside him at Crecy. Such a glittering and exalted assembly was a rare thing in Cornwall and was to become rarer, for after his death the Dukedom reverted to the

Restormel Castle in ruins in the eighteenth century

throne. Within a few years, the four great Norman castles began to fall into decay; Restormel became a crumbling ruin whilst Launceston. Tintagel and Trematon were maintained only as prisons.

In 1453 the Hundred Years War was over, with only Calais left in English hands and at once thirty years of civil war began, now known as the Wars of the Roses. In 1485 these too were over, with the Lancastrian Henry Tudor on the throne. The Cornish gentry generally had supported him in the struggle and were duly rewarded. The Fowey Gallants, the men of Looe and other longshoremen of the south coast had continued to prosper both on legitimate trade with France and on piracy during these unsettled years but those on the land, as well as the tinners, were weary of taxes for purposes of distant wars. They rebelled, marching almost as far as London – to be savagely and murderously suppressed in 1497 by their new Tudor king. But far more momentous events were to follow; in 1509 Henry VIII came to the throne and it was he who set under way the Reformation in England, a religious revolution which was grievously to affect the Cornish people.

5

The Reformation to the Civil War

Barely ten years after the beginning of the Hundred Years War, disaster had struck England. This was the terrible pestilence called the Plague, or Black Death. Living conditions in Cornwall were no better than elsewhere in the country and the disease, thriving on the presence of filth, fleas and rats, caused the death of something like one third of the already small population during 1348-9. One of the effects of this epidemic was that it put an end to the sporadic church building that had been going on throughout the county, chiefly additions and alterations to the buildings which the Normans had erected. This sudden halt in activity was partly due to a lack of stone masons and other craftsmen and it was not for another forty or fifty years that building started again.

This rebuilding began with great religious fervour and enthusiasm, and nearly all the parish churches were enlarged or altered during the later fifteenth and early sixteenth centuries, in the new Perpendicular style. By about 1530 most churches, however small, had been richly decorated within, and sometimes without, with a love and devotion which most of us today would find difficult to comprehend. For instance, the exterior walls of the churches at Launceston and Truro were elaborately carved, while the interior of almost every church was given a beautifully carved and sumptuously coloured barrel roof, a gilded and painted Rood and screen, richly glowing stained glass windows like those remaining at St. Neot, and carved bench ends of oak. The interior walls were usually covered with colourful paintings instructing the illiterate but devout Roman Catholic peasants of Cornwall in the Bible, much as a child is given a picture book before it can read.

Then, in 1534, because the Pope refused to grant Henry VIII a divorce from Katherine of Aragon, the English king severed this country from the church of Rome, declaring himself supreme head of the Church of England. Thereupon the Pope excommunicated him, and Henry replied by dissolving the monasteries. In Cornwall this meant the break-up of the wealthy and important priories of Bodmin, Launceston and St. Germans as well as other smaller houses. This did not affect the common people greatly and indeed the monasteries generally were regarded as having outlived their useful purpose; the county gentry, strongly Catholic or no, bought up the monastic lands in businesslike fashion and so added to their estates. The money from this, as well as the wealth from the monasteries, went to fill the royal coffers. Out of these, at a later date, St. Mawes and Pendennis castles were built, to strengthen the Channel defences.

This then was the beginning of the Reformation in England, which after Henry's death was carried on by more ruthless hands, for while he had remained a Catholic – though not a Roman Catholic – to the end, his successor was a convinced Protestant. Thus, to the anguish of the Cornish people, attention was turned next to their parish churches and the ritual which they knew so well. The time-honoured Latin mass was abolished and a simpler service in English, as laid down in the new English Book of Common Prayer, was enforced upon

St Mawes Castle, built by Henry VIII

them. No longer were they even allowed to use Cornish for the Lord's Prayer, the Creed and Ten Commandments as the Roman church had wisely permitted them to do and, as many of them understood no English, the new service was totally unintelligible to them. In addition all images were forcibly removed from the churches, the first step in a large-scale plunder, whilst the use of holy water and holy bread was forbidden, among other things.

The Cornish people and those of Devon were so angry that in 1549 six thousand besieged Exeter in the Prayer Book Rebellion, and thence sent their demands to London for the restoration of the Latin service and the ritual which they loved. But their cause was hopeless and, lacking even the support of the gentry – now largely Protestant – they were quickly defeated and their leaders put to death in barbarous fashion. A year later began a wholesale destruction or confiscation of all the lovely things in their churches, costly plate and vestments, stained glass, pictures and statues, even the church bells and Cornish crosses. Eventually, under threat of severe fine, the people perforce continued to fill the churches, now colourless and bare, stripped of all which had claimed their love and obedience and around which their lives had revolved. And, moreover, to listen to the foreign tongue of those they heartily disliked. It was this more than anything else which brought about the disappearance of the Cornish tongue, together with the almost total destruction of the only writings in the language – religious manuscripts in the possession of the monasteries.

It was not long before Protestant England was at logger-heads with the might of Catholic Spain, whose devout ruler wanted England brought back into the Church of Rome. Cornwall, at the approaches to the English Channel, suddenly became of great strategic importance and, although neither monarch wanted war, it was not long before the seafarers of the south-western peninsula took matters into their own hands. They waged war at sea with Spain unofficially, and yet not entirely without the approval of Elizabeth, who managed to turn a blind eye to most of their exploits. Thousands of seamen, spurred on by their love of adventure and the Queen, their hatred of the Pope and the foreigner, made profit, even fortunes out of these buccaneering activities; their names included the famous, like Drake and Hawkins, and the less celebrated, such as the infamous pirate Killigrews of Falmouth. The small ports of this remote corner of England stood in the front line during this period of cold war and saw much exciting activity as little ships on voyages of piracy, privateering, trading or discovery set forth; they left at their owners' risk and expense, to intercept Spanish ships laden with Peruvian treasure on the high seas, to raid Spanish settlements in the New World, impudently to ship African slaves to the mines and plantations of Spanish settlers in central America – a lucrative trade this, instigated by Drake and Hawkins – and to harry ships in the Channel running between the wealthy Spanish Netherlands and the mother country.

When in 1585 war with Spain was openly declared, Cornwall was still in the van of battle. Elizabeth at once made Raleigh Lord Warden of the Stannaries and then Lord Lieutenant of the county, with his cousin Grenville, of the great Cornish family, as supervisor of Cornwall's defences. Along the coast warning beacons were prepared for the expected invasion, the peasantry were given brief and inadequate military training, and coastal defences were erected in all possible landing places, at Falmouth in particular. In 1588 the long anticipated Spanish Armada, advancing in a great crescent of 130 galleons with 20,000 of the best troops in Europe aboard, was first sighted off Scilly. It sailed slowly past the Cornish coast; off Dodman Head the ships dropped sail for a council of war; at Cawsand two were disabled in a skirmish with the English; and the Armada's commander, it is said, cast envious eyes towards Mount Edgcumbe, the lovely house by Plymouth Sound, which he knew and where he intended to live after victory. But the English fleet, including ships owned, commanded or manned by Cornishmen, outmanoeuvred the crescent of clumsy galleons, which had proposed to encircle them, and dispersed the Spanish in the North Sea. For a brief time Cornwall felt at ease, but there were two other Armadas in 1596 and 1597, both scattered by gales before they reached her shores. The last had been bound for Falmouth and the castle of Pendennis. Meanwhile there had been several successful Spanish raids from occupied Brittany; Mousehole, Newlyn and Penzance were actually sacked and burned in

1595 before Drake appeared and the Spanish fled down Channel.

Inevitably the events of the Reformation in Cornwall, as elsewhere, produced not only some who became more ardent Catholics than before but others who thought that the movement had not gone far enough, and wished to rid the Church of England of 'popishness', of archbishops, bishops and elaborate ceremony. These were the Puritans, who, in the end, became persecuted by Elizabeth, by James I, her successor and by his heir, Charles I. During James' reign, many fled to the New World; the Pilgrim Fathers, for instance, set sail along the Cornish coast from Plymouth in 1620. But during Charles' reign, matters became even more serious. Initially a quarrel began between the monarch and his Parliament over his unconstitutional behaviour raising money by forced loan, for example, without their consent. Several Cornish gentry, refusing to pay, were imprisioned or otherwise punished. Their able leader in the House of Commons, Sir John Eliot of Port Eliot in east Cornwall, was eventually imprisoned in the Tower, where he died. The dispute, therefore, was really as to who in the state was supreme, king or Parliament, but it soon resolved itself into more than that and the Great Civil War of 1642 began, with those who supported the *status quo* in the Church on the king's side and with the Puritans on the other. Many found it difficult to take sides, and in Cornwall a number of the great families were divided amongst themselves. The leading men of the day, however, such as Sir John Arundell, Sir Bevil Grenville, Sir Richard Vyvyan and Sir Francis Godolphin were Royalists, as was the county as a whole. East Cornwall, like Devon, was more Puritan.

One of the most remarkable features of the war was the forming of a Cornish army by the leading Royalist gentry who, after the first six months, had found the local militia inadequate. Comprised chiefly of their own tenants, courageous, disciplined and devoted to its commanders, this little army fought successful battles at Braddock Down near Lostwithiel, holding the well trained Roundheads at bay, and again at Stratton near Bude in 1643. It then moved up-country and so courageously assisted in the capture of Bristol and Exeter that the king put its valour on permanent record by issuing an address thanking the Cornish for their services.

The island fortress of St Michael's Mount

By the end of this campaign, the Cornish army had lost its four greatest leaders and thereafter was never the same again. Discipline and morale, as well as the spirit of its new commanders, all diminished and in 1645 matters grew worse with the swift advance westwards of Cromwell's New Model Army. The last royalist strongholds in Cornwall were Pendennis Castle and St. Michael's Mount. The island fort surrendered in April 1645 and Pendennis in August, after a siege lasting five months and with starvation near at hand. It was Arundell who led out the garrison with 'colours flying, trumpets sounding, drums beating', and spirits still high.

But the Cornish people as a whole were war weary and impoverished. And worse was to come. First, in the far west famine, the Plague and then throughout the county, another pestilence in the form of over-zealous Puritans who busied themselves 'purifying' the churches even further by destroying what little remained of their mediaeval splendour – whitewashing the inner walls and their mural paintings, shattering stained glass, tearing down Rood screens and generally destroying such statues and other treasures as had escaped earlier destruction. It is not surprising that by the end of the seventeenth century many Cornish people were ceasing to go to church at all.

6

The Industrial Revolution and Beyond

During the late sixteenth and early seventeenth centuries, before the first stirrings of industrial revolution in England, the appearance and economy of Cornwall were little changed from the Middle Ages. The staple exports were tin and pilchards and those engaged in these industries formed slightly greater concentrations of population in an area very sparsely peopled and largely agricultural. Along the coast were a number of thriving fishing villages, Mevagissey, Polperro, Port Isaac and Mousehole, for instance, where the industry was on an organised basis. Their occupants depended for a livelihood upon the seasonal arrival of the pilchard shoals into in-shore waters, and upon their successful salting down by the tens of thousands, The fish was of vital importance in the economy, forming the basic diet of Cornwall's hungry poor and providing a growing export trade to the Roman Catholic countries of Europe, where it was consumed during Lent.

As for tin, production had gradually shifted westwards, so that while Penzance became a coinage town in 1663, Liskeard and Lostwithiel were by that date declining. Until about 1700 the metal was still being obtained almost wholly from alluvial deposits; but lode mining had commenced and it is probable that among the first such mines were those around St. Just and on the north coast near St. Agnes. In both these localities, the workings could be drained without the use of machinery, by driving adits, or drainage tunnels, into the cliffs. Where drainage by adit was not possible other methods had to be used, including crude hand pumps of various kinds, whilst waterwheels were later introduced to drain mine workings less fortunately placed. Then, at the beginning of the eighteenth century, the first atmospheric pumping engines, using the power of steam, made their appearance. The first of these, it is believed, was erected on the rich tin mine known as Wheal Vor near Helston, about 1715. The next four were installed on copper mines, three of which were near Chacewater. This fact is significant for it signalled the

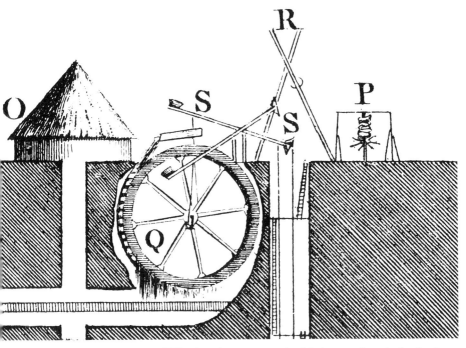

Diagram dated 1778, showing a waterwheel being used to drain the deep levels of a copper mine instead of a steam engine; note the primitive derrick, capstan and ladders

beginnings of a new industry for Cornwall, copper mining, which was rapidly to outstrip that of tin in importance and was to be of much more value to the county for more than a century to come. Cornwall became, in fact, the principal copper producer in the world for some decades. The first mines sprang up in the area between Chacewater and Redruth, and as their output grew so did the population. Before long this area had become the most densely populated part of the county.

The life of this new breed of Cornish miners, men who worked underground unlike the older streamers on the surface workings, was very different and of a much harsher nature. The deeper the mines became, the more working conditions worsened, the men having to contend with excessive heat and humidity, insanitary and dangerous surroundings, and long hours of strenuous labour. This included climbing down and up ladders to and from their pitches far underground. A return home at the end of a tiring core, or shift, brought small improvement, for the hundreds of small hovels which mushroomed in the mining districts were all usually built by the miners themselves and were damp and overcrowded. Among the labouring poor there was little comfort. The miner, like the fisherman and farm worker, more often than not sought solace in drinking beer or smuggled spirits, and occupied his few leisure hours with such brutish pastimes as cock-fighting, bull-baiting and the grim business of wrecking.

It was among these hard drinking and lawless tinners that John Wesley came in 1743, riding down into this backward corner of Britain in the hope of breathing fresh life into a church which the Reformation had all but put to death. Few of the lower orders of Cornishmen attended church with enthusiasm and fewer still cared that this was so. In fact many of the clergy held more than one living, thus doubling or even trebling their stipends, while being absent from one or other

Gwennap pit, scene of annual Methodist rallies on Whit Mondays; this photograph is from about 1900

of their parishes for months at a time. People were often at a loss for help when it came to burials, baptisms and marriages.

Wesley, with his brother and others, visited Cornwall almost every year until 1789, spending most of his time amongst the mining districts although no part of the county was neglected by him. The simple Cornish people, at heart deeply religious and sadly in need of guidance from the church, were soon won over by the preaching and teaching of Wesley and could not but admire the way in which he toiled among them from dawn to dusk, often when hungry, wet and tired from his travels from parish to parish on horseback. By the time of Wesley's last journey in 1789 numerous 'preaching houses' or chapels had been erected and in these primitive little buildings, often the work of the village people themselves, Methodism took firm hold in the county. Once again the Cornish were keen churchgoers.

It must have been during the early 1800s that the famous Cornish toast 'Fish, tin and copper' came into being, for by this time the new branch of the age-old mining industry was the staple of Cornwall, bringing with it the full impetus of the Industrial Revolution. In addition to the mines around Redruth, further rich deposits of copper ore were found near St. Austell and on Caradon Hill north of Liskeard, while the Land's End tin mines were still active. The landscape of these mining areas at this period was dominated by the massive houses containing beam engines whose task it was to work pumps to drain the underground workings, or else to draw ores to surface. The ores were carried off the mines by teams of pack mules, tin to the nearest blowing or smelting house and copper ore to the coast, since this was shipped off for smelting in South Wales, where coal was available in quantity. As output of copper soared, the Cornish ports handling the trade grew apace, and some of them acquired mineral railways or tramroads to serve the local mines as well.

In many ways this first half of the nineteenth century was the halcyon age for Cornwall and marked the peak of her industrial might, until the collapse of the copper mining industry about 1865 in the face of severe foreign competition. Numbers of mineral landlords, smelters, mine merchants and

Opposite: an optimistic share prospectus

FREE EMIGRATION
To Port Adelaide, in South Australia.

EVERY kind of LABORER and ARTIZAN may, if married, of good character, and within the age prescribed by the Commissioners, obtain a free passage to this flourishing colony, by applying on or before SATURDAY next, the 14th of September instant, to

Mr. I. LATIMER,
ROSEWYN ROW, TRURO.

This colony is well *watered;* by reference to a map it will be seen that the river Torrens flows between the two portions of the city of *Adelaide,* and the river Murray is very near it. This river has been termed the Mississippi of Australia : already it has been traced more than 1000 miles.

The Advertiser wishes to direct the especial attention of the Public to this fact, that all that the BISHOP of EXETER is now saying about Australia, to the country, in his Cantge, has *to reference to South Australia,* but chiefly to *New South Wales,* which is but a small portion, comparatively, of that vast continent ; and all that Mr. WILBERFORCE says about the vice and demoralization of *Australia,* has reference only to the penal settlements of *New South Wales, Van Diemens Land,* and *Norfolk Island.* Only the former country belongs to *Australia* ; and why the Right Rev. Prelate and the Rev. Gentleman are not more accurate in the use of their terms must be left for the consideration of the Public. The morality of the colony of *South* Australia is secured in every way that can be thought of ; no emigrant is sent there whose testimonials as to character, health, &c. are not signed by two householders, a physician or surgeon, the minister of his parish, or one of the local magistrates.

Mr. Latimer will be happy to give any information on the subject, and supply the work of any author who has written on this country, having copies of nearly the whole of the works that have appeared on South Australia always in his possesion.

From the West Briton, *1839*

adventurers made fortunes. These, the well-to-do, divided their lives between their country seats, many of which were rebuilt out of fortunes made in mining, and new town houses in places such as Falmouth, Bodmin and Truro. This was especially the case in Truro where a surprisingly elegant social 'season' could be enjoyed. As for the labouring poor, concentrated in thriving new mining centres such as Camborne, St. Day and Lanner, at least there was plentiful work, however bad the conditions underground, and they were soon to look back on this state of affairs with some nostalgia when the mining slump came.

There was a brief revival in the fortunes of tin mining in the 1870s and then like copper, although less swiftly, the industry fell into ruins. One after another scores of mines were closed down, with pumping ceased and the waters rising in the shafts as if to seal their fate for ever. Then began the slow decay of dozens of giant engine-houses and the more rapid deterioration of the scores of miners' cottages of cob and thatch. Their owners departed to seek work in mines and mining camps in the far corners of the globe – the emigrant Cornish miners known as Cousin Jacks who were to become familiar in Australia, South Africa and much of the Americas. Settlements in Cornwall such as St. Day and St. Just became ghosts of their former selves. Lucky was the family which had not at least one member, usually the young and strong, abroad – or unlucky perhaps, since the need for money sent home by these exiled Cornishmen took precedence over the miseries of separation.

In addition to the great depression in mining, another economic disaster of only a little less magnitude struck the county towards the end of the nineteenth century. The pilchard, which for so long had been one of the staples of the Cornishman's diet and had provided so much employment along the county's seaboard, ceased to come in-shore in shoals at the end of each summer as it once had done. Thereafter the

The pilchard fleet setting out from St Ives, about 1900

pilchard fishing industry began to die a slow death, though supported to some extent by a change to fishing for mackerel.

Fortunately as the two great industries of the past declined, others developed which were in part able to offset the worst economic effects. The foundations were laid for a new and better future, although few in the mining and fishing industries in those depressed days could see it.

There was, for instance, the first interest shown in the county as a place to visit for summer sea-bathing or as an escape from the rigours of the English winter up-country. Several coastal towns were beginning to experience the first small influx of these visitors, particularly Penzance, which above all enjoyed a mild winter climate. Inevitably, the numbers of these early holiday makers were not great for the primitive state of the roads there, as well as its remoteness, made any journey to Cornwall a prolonged and uncomfortable experience. It took 40 hours to reach Falmouth from London by stage coach.

Horse buses such as this from Helston to Cury and Mullion, here used for a wedding party, became even more important after the coming of railways

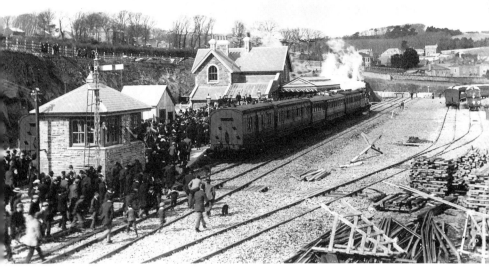

The opening of Padstow Station, 27 March 1899

From about 1820, during the years of Cornwall's great mining prosperity, the road system had been improved radically; but of greater importance to the future was the introduction and gradual spread of railways. The various lines were intended at the outset primarily for mineral traffic and were thus concentrated within the mining districts but provision for passengers was soon to follow. In 1846 the West Cornwall Railway was formed to take over and extend to Truro and Penzance the old Hayle Railway which had been built earlier from the port of Hayle to the Redruth mines. A year later the Cornwall Railway was promoted, to build a line from Truro to Plymouth. As it happened, the railway-building mania in the county, which had produced so many small mineral and other projected lines, was really over by this date and both these new Cornish railways were slow in completion. It was not until 1859, when Brunel's impressive bridge over the Tamar was opened, that it was possible to travel by rail down the length of the county to Penzance.

The most significant users of this new artery through Cornwall, however, were not passengers at all. Within a year or two the daily goods traffic moving up to London included fish – chiefly mackerel caught by the Mount's Bay drifters –

potatoes and broccoli; all were commodities of which Cornwall could produce plenty once wider markets were brought within easy reach. For many years the mackerel boats brought in vast quantities of fish, while the market gardening industry, especially in the Mount's Bay area and around the Fal estuary had become of great importance. The reason is, of course, that spring comes early to Cornwall so that Cornish potatoes as well as other vegetables appeared on the London market weeks ahead of any other, thus commanding high prices.

If springtime is early in Cornwall it arrives even sooner in the Isles of Scilly. These clustered granite isles have little to offer man, and life there had always been a struggle. Until the 1830s the principal source of income, apart from smuggling, had been kelp (calcined ashes of seaweed) which was shipped to Bristol to make glass and soap. When this trade ceased, due to the development of alternative sources of supply, the islands fell upon very hard times indeed. Then in 1871, another significant consignment travelled up to London by rail, consisting of a hatbox filled with cut flowers for the Covent Garden market. This trial sale, an astonishing success, was the beginning of a flourishing industry in spring flowers which depended entirely upon the early spring and lack of frost which Scilly enjoys at a time when up-country buyers are still trapped in the cold and gloom of winter. Today flowers are carried to Penzance on the *Scillonian* by the thousands of tons and thence again by the all important railway to London.

Together with horticulture, the growing of flowers, which has spread onto the mainland, was to become one of the three staple industries of modern Cornwall, although with the twentieth century it was to be outstripped by the tourist industry. On the main line, swifter and more frequent trains meant a rapid increase in the number of summer visitors after the turn of the century, whilst branch lines distributed them to the up-and-coming resorts such as Newquay, Perranporth, St. Ives, Falmouth, Fowey and Looe. Their annual arrival was to prove the salvation of many of these towns, whose livelihood from fishing had so drastically fallen away and whose occupants now were beginning to see themselves in a new light. The sandy sheltered bays and rocky coasts from which they had wrested a living became translated into bathing

Building Truro Cathedral, about 1890

beaches and scenic coastline, their formerly rather unsalubrious fishing villages into quaint tourist attractions.

It is a strange fact that most of the holidaymakers who constitute one of the two main industries of Cornwall visit the county without being aware of the presence of the other. This is the production of china clay, the thriving modern industry which had its beginnings in the early nineteenth century but which remained virtually in obscurity until about the 1870s. Originally the white clay, or kaolin, was used entirely in the manufacture of pottery and it was Staffordshire potters who owned the first shallow pits on the Hensbarrow granite behind St Austell. The kaolin, which is a constituent of decomposed granite, was separated out from unwanted waste matter by the use of running water and basically that is still the principle of extraction today. In the interim the industry has grown to very considerable proportions, as have the white cones of waste quartz which typify the landscape of the china clay country.

With the development of new techniques, production increased enormously during the closing years of the nineteenth century. By 1912 annual production was in excess of 850,000 tons. There were growing demands from the paper making, chemical and paint industries as well as the traditional pottery industry.

The twentieth century has seen many changes. China clay is now the leading mining industry; copper has gone for good and tin will only be viable when the world prices rise, and then only in a relatively small way. Fishing remains important, but not on the previous scale. The rapidly expanding tourist industry has created new jobs and revived old, but inevitably it has also brought problems.

The huge influx of visitors and new residents from up-country have been factors in the dilution of Cornish culture and customs. Many feel it is imperative to retain and restore that culture which made the Cornish people and their land unique. The toast of 'Fish, tin and copper' may be heard no more, but the spirit lives on in all the Cornish.

Cornwall for ever
Kernow bys vyken